CRADLED IN GRACE

Cradled in Grace

CHARLEY WHITE

Contents

For Eric, Bentley & Hartley Ann
Love you more than Buttered Toast!

In memory of those I get to love on the
other side of Heaven:

Eliza Jane, Thomas Walker, Clara Dean

A Sacred Grief

Grief is a universal human experience, yet for many women, the grief of pre-birth loss—miscarriage, stillbirth, or pre-term death—is often a silent and isolating sorrow. It is a grief that exists in the realm of "what might have been," deeply personal and often misunderstood. While society may dismiss or minimize this loss, its impact leaves an indelible mark on the soul of the mother.

For a body of believers called to rejoice with those who rejoice and weep with those who weep (Romans 12:15), the church's silence on pre-birth loss is deeply troubling. The very institution that proclaims the sanctity of life often struggles to acknowledge the sacredness of lives lost unseen. This silence amplifies the pain, leaving grieving parents to carry their sorrow alone.

As a mother who has experienced three miscarriages, I know this pain intimately. My first loss came during a tumultuous period in my life—unmarried, in an abusive relationship, and wholly unprepared for motherhood. Yet, when I saw the positive pregnancy test, something shifted. I was not just a struggling young woman; I was a mother. Losing that child shattered me, yet shame and fear kept me silent. I believed my grief was not valid, a mindset shaped by a culture of judgment rather than grace.

Years later, two more losses followed in the first year of my marriage—a time when I eagerly prayed for children. These miscarriages brought a different kind of grief, compounded by confusion and questioning. I turned to the church for solace, only to find its silence deafening. The institution that celebrates life in the womb had no space for mourning its loss, leaving me to navigate my sorrow with little guidance.

This silence is not just a personal experience; it is a systemic issue. By failing to address pre-birth loss, the church risks sending an unintended message: that these lives are less sacred, less worthy of mourning. This contradiction undermines the church's witness and leaves a void that society fills with narratives diminishing the value of life in the womb.

Yet Scripture paints a different picture. In Psalm 139, David declares, "You knit me together in my mother's womb... I am fearfully and wonderfully made" (Ps. 139:13-14). Jeremiah 1:5 echoes this truth: "Before I formed you in the womb, I knew you; before you were born, I set you apart." These verses affirm that every life, no matter how brief, is precious to God.

This book is both a call to action and a source of hope. It is a call for the church to embrace those who grieve pre-birth loss, offering compassion and acknowledgment. And it is a reminder to grieving parents that their pain is seen, their loss is valid, and their children are cherished by the Creator.

How has silence shaped your understanding of grief—your own or others? What steps can you take to ensure that silence is replaced with compassion and acknowledgment, especially within your faith community?

Chapter One

Silent Grief

Grief is often described as a universal human experience, yet when it comes to pre-birth loss, the nature of grief becomes uniquely profound. For many, this type of loss is compounded by a lack of societal acknowledgment. Miscarriage and stillbirth are frequently experienced in silence, leaving a void where public mourning spaces should exist. This isolation can intensify the grieving process, making it feel deeply personal yet invisibly burdensome.

According to the American Pregnancy Association, up to 20% of known pregnancies end in miscarriage. While this statistic underscores the prevalence of the experience, it cannot capture the depth of the emotional toll. The grief accompanying the loss of a child at any stage is profound, encompassing emotional, physical, and spiritual dimensions that can endure for years. Often, this grief is classified as "ambiguous loss," a term coined by Dr. Pauline Boss to describe losses that are not clearly defined or socially acknowledged. Miscarriage and stillbirth exemplify this type of loss, as they frequently lack the societal rituals of mourning that validate other forms of bereavement. As a result, women may feel emotionally abandoned and spiritually alone, their grief unrecognized and misunderstood.

The psychological impact of pre-birth loss is significant. Studies published in *Obstetrics & Gynecology* reveal that up to 20% of women who experience miscarriage suffer from depression or PTSD, with 20-30% developing anxiety disorders. These effects can persist for months or even years, intertwining with feelings of guilt and the profound loss of a future once envisioned. Unlike other forms of grief, the absence of public acknowledgment—such as funerals—can leave women feeling that their pain is less valid. Many report feeling forgotten by friends, family, and even their faith communities, further isolating them in their suffering.

Personal stories reveal the complex layers of this grief. One woman shared: "After my miscarriage, I felt like no one understood the pain I was going through. It was like I had lost a part of myself, but no one could see it. People would tell me to 'move on' or 'try again,' but those words only deepened the wound. I couldn't move on. I couldn't forget the child I had already loved. The grief was so heavy, and yet, I felt like I couldn't talk about it." This story echoes the experiences of countless women who feel dismissed by a culture that prioritizes forward momentum over the acknowledgment of loss.

Another mother's account highlights the spiritual conflict many women endure: "I prayed for this child. I believed so strongly that God would protect him and bring him safely into the world. When I delivered him stillborn, I couldn't understand why. I felt angry with God. I questioned everything I had believed in. My faith felt so fragile in that moment. I didn't know if I could ever trust again." For many, the spiritual toll of pre-birth loss includes feelings of betrayal and doubt, compounding the pain with a crisis of faith.

Relationships within families also suffer under the strain of pre-birth loss. Marriages are often tested as couples grapple with their grief in disparate ways. One woman shared: "We were both devastated by the loss of our baby, but I felt like my husband wasn't grieving in the same way. I wanted him to cry with me, to mourn with me. But he wasn't, and I felt so alone. We never talked about it in the way I needed to. It was like we were grieving separately, even though we were both hurting deeply." Men and women often process grief differently, which can lead to frustration and misunderstanding. For some couples, this dissonance creates distance, while others find a path to deeper connection through shared vulnerability.

My personal journey through pre-birth loss brought me to a place of profound darkness. After losing two children with my husband, I descended into a depression so painful that I contemplated ending my life. My husband, in his way of coping, poured himself into his work, striving to provide for our future. To my grieving heart, his efforts felt like avoidance, as though he failed to acknowledge our shared loss. I could not see that his busyness was a manifestation of his grief—a way to manage his pain and his fear of losing me to despair. Our unspoken hurts became an undercurrent in our marriage, surfacing in arguments and unfulfilled expectations. For nearly a decade, this unaddressed sorrow lingered, allowing the enemy to exploit our vulnerability and deepen the wounds.

The church's silence on pre-birth loss further isolates grieving women. One woman recounted: "I remember going to church a few weeks after my miscarriage and hoping someone would acknowledge my loss. But no one said anything. No prayers, no comfort, no kind words. It was as if my grief didn't exist. I wanted them to see that my baby was real, that I was hurting, but instead, I was left to grieve quietly." The lack of acknowledgment from faith communities compounds the pain, leaving women to question whether their grief is justified or whether they are expected to "move on" without support.

Despite the heavy toll, many women find paths to healing. One mother shared: "It took me a long time to come to peace with the loss of my baby. Some days, I felt like I was moving forward, and others, I was overwhelmed by sadness. Over time, I learned it was okay to grieve on my own timeline. Talking with other women who had similar experiences helped me feel less alone. Slowly, I began to heal, finding a deeper compassion for others." For many, support groups—whether in person or online—offer a safe space to share stories and find understanding.

The grief of pre-birth loss is profound and often invisible, but it is no less real than any other form of loss. Women need spaces to grieve openly, with compassion and understanding from their communities. Acknowledging this grief is vital—not only for individual healing but also for the collective strength of families and faith communities. Only when we give voice to this pain can we begin the journey toward healing.

In what ways have you experienced or observed the silence of the church surrounding pre-birth loss, and how might acknowledging this grief open the door for deeper healing and connection within the body of Christ?

Chapter Two

The Sanctity of Life

Life begins with a sacred whisper—a heartbeat, a spark, a divine creation. For mothers who have experienced pre-birth loss, this truth becomes deeply personal, a thread of hope to cling to in the midst of sorrow. The belief that life is precious, even from its earliest moments, can offer comfort and assurance that every child, no matter how brief their time, is cherished by God. For me, this truth became all the more meaningful after losing my own children, as I clung to the belief that their lives were sacred and purposeful, regardless of how brief they were.

The psalmist beautifully captures this truth in Psalm 139:13-16: "For you created my inmost being; you knit me together in my mother's womb. I praise you because I am fearfully and wonderfully made; your works are wonderful, I know that full well. My frame was not hidden from you when I was made in the secret place, when I was woven together in the depths of the earth. Your eyes saw my unformed body; all the days ordained for me were written in your book before one of them came to be." These verses affirm that each life, no matter how short, is lovingly formed by God and known in its entirety by Him. For grieving mothers, including myself, these words serve as a reminder that my children's existence, though fleeting, was purposeful and sacred.

When I experienced my first miscarriage, I felt a sense of loss and confusion, but also an undeniable connection to the child I had lost. I knew, deep in my heart, that I had lost a daughter. It wasn't something that could be explained by science or logic, but it was a gut instinct I carried with me. Later, when my husband and I had the DNA tests done after my first miscarriage, it revealed that the child we had lost had been a boy. The revelation wasn't as surprising to me as it might have been to others, because I had felt all along that this child was meant to be with us for a time, and I knew that the child's existence mattered to God.

When I had a third miscarriage, I believed once again that I had lost a girl. This belief became a part of my mourning, helping me to name the loss, to honor that precious life, and to connect with it in a deeper way. Through the pain, I also experienced a kind of sacred knowing—that the child, though not visible to the world, was still loved, still precious, and still known by the Creator.

The turning point came during a counseling session at my church, when I was asked if I had ever considered naming my unborn children. The question caught me off guard, but it also stirred something deep within me. I had never thought about naming them in a formal way before, but that night, after the session, my husband and I sat together and spoke about those three children—our children in heaven. Through tears and shared memories, we named them. It felt like an act of reclaiming their existence, of honoring their sacredness. Naming them was a way to say, "You were here, and you mattered." We made a promise to ourselves and to God that their names would live on, that they would not be forgotten, and that we would honor them as part of our family.

One of the first things I did when we moved into our current home was purchase three large prints for our hallway. Each print depicts Jesus walking individually with each of our children, in their own sacred space with Him. It's a visual reminder in our home that our children are not lost, but cherished and held by the Savior. They may not walk this earth with us, but in our hearts and in our home, they have a place.

We also talk to our living children about their older siblings in heaven. They know their names and understand that these siblings are waiting for us. It is important to me that our living children know that their older siblings are real, and that their lives matter. These conversations, though sometimes difficult, are also healing. They serve as a reminder that life is precious from the very beginning, and even though we may not fully understand the reasons for loss, we can trust that God's plan is perfect, and that our children, though not with us in this life, are with Him in eternity.

The calling of the prophet Jeremiah echoes this tender truth. In Jeremiah 1:5, God declares, "Before I formed you in the womb I knew you, before you were born I set you apart." Such divine intimacy assures us that each child is known and loved by God from the very beginning. This knowledge can bring solace to mothers, affirming that their child's life was intentional and precious in the eyes of the Creator. For my own experience, this truth was a source of comfort. I knew, without a doubt, that God knew my children, that their existence was not a fluke, but part of His perfect plan. Their lives, though short, were woven into the tapestry of God's will.

As Christians, we believe that every human being is created in the image of God, the Imago Dei (Genesis 1:27). This belief underscores the inherent value of every life, regardless of its duration or circumstances. For mothers grieving pre-birth loss, this truth can transform sorrow into a sacred honor—recognizing their child as a reflection of God's creative power and love. Their grief, while profound, becomes a testament to the depth of love they carried for the life they nurtured. This was true for me. Each of my children, though not here with me in this life, is an eternal reflection of God's love.

Yet, for many mothers, the silence surrounding pre-birth loss within faith communities can add to their heartache. Too often, the absence of acknowledgment leaves them feeling alone in their grief. When I lost my children, I longed for the church to see, to recognize, to affirm that the lives of my children, no matter how short, mattered. But often, there was silence. The silence felt like an erasure of their existence, and in that silence, the pain was compounded. The church has a unique opportunity to step into this space, to affirm the sanctity of life from its very beginning, and to walk alongside mothers in their journey of healing. The smallest acts—a prayer, a word of comfort, a memorial service—can make all the difference, reminding grieving families that their loss is seen and their child's life is valued.

Hope is a light that shines through the darkness of grief, and the promise of eternal life offers a profound comfort to mothers who have lost a child. Jesus assures us in John 14:2-3: "My Father's house has many rooms; if that were not so, would I have told you that I am going there to prepare a place for you? And if I go and prepare a place for you, I will come back and take you to be with me that you also may be where I am." This promise extends to the children lost before birth, offering a vision of reunion and peace. The thought of being reunited with my children one day brings immeasurable comfort.

King David's words in 2 Samuel 12:23 provide a poignant glimpse into this hope. After losing his infant son, David said, "But now that he is dead, why should I go on fasting? Can I bring him back again? I will go to him, but he will not return to me." David's confidence in being reunited with his child reflects the hope available to all who trust in God's promises. For grieving mothers, this assurance can transform their sorrow into anticipation, knowing their child rests safely in the presence of the Creator.

Recognizing the sanctity of life before birth calls us to honor every life, both in its presence and in its loss. For mothers, this acknowledgment can be a turning point—affirming the sacredness of their child's existence and offering both validation of their grief and the promise of reunion. The church plays a vital role in upholding these truths, creating spaces where mourning is met with grace and healing.

Every life, no matter how small or short, reflects the handiwork of God. For mothers who mourn, the knowledge that their child was lovingly created and deeply known offers a foundation for healing and a lens to see their child's life as a cherished part of God's eternal plan. In this sacred understanding, grief is met with hope, and sorrow becomes a testament to the depth of love—a love that echoes the Creator's own.

How can you honor the memory of your lost child in a way that affirms their sacred value and keeps their life woven into your family's story?

Chapter Three

The Cost of Silence

The silence surrounding pre-birth loss within the church isn't just the absence of words, but often the presence of words that fail to meet the weight of a mother's grief. In my experience, the church's attempts to offer comfort were often laced with well-meaning but ultimately hollow platitudes—phrases like "God needed another angel" or "It's all part of God's plan." These words, though said with the intention of soothing, ended up cutting deeper, leaving me feeling more isolated in my sorrow.

But the impact of the church's silence goes beyond the immediate sting of poorly chosen words. It reflects a broader cultural discomfort with grief itself, especially the grief that comes from pre-birth loss. In many religious settings, the silence surrounding this type of loss is not simply a matter of being unsure of what to say—it's a cultural issue rooted in our collective discomfort with death and mourning. The church, like much of society, often struggles to face the harsh reality of loss and suffering. There's a tendency to want to rush through it, to find an explanation or a silver lining, rather than allowing the grief to sit, raw and real. This discomfort can lead to a deeper psychological impact on those who are grieving. When grief is minimized or brushed aside, the psychological burden on the mourner is compounded. It creates a sense of isolation and alienation, as though the loss itself is too painful to acknowledge in full.

This cultural avoidance of deep, uncomfortable grief often results in a lack of empathy. The church, rather than providing a space to honor the sacredness of pre-birth loss, can unintentionally communicate that this grief is somehow less legitimate than other forms of mourning. By failing to recognize the deep pain of mothers who have lost a child before birth, the church creates an environment where that pain is not validated. It sends the message that the child, though deeply loved, is somehow less significant because they were never seen by the world. This type of silence creates an invisible grief—a grief that is not only unspoken but also unrecognized.

The psychological toll of this silence is significant. When a mother is told that her child's life is part of God's plan or that she will see her child again in heaven, it can feel dismissive, like her grief is being invalidated or hurried along. These well-meaning statements are often rooted in an attempt to relieve the suffering, but they don't allow space for the grief to be fully experienced. The result is a sense of emotional disconnection—not just from others but from one's own feelings of loss. Grieving mothers may begin to question their own emotions, feeling that their sorrow is inappropriate or that they should be moving on faster. This can lead to feelings of guilt, shame, and confusion about how to grieve in a way that feels right.

Moreover, when the church fails to create a space for mourning, it perpetuates a cycle of silence that extends beyond the individual mother. It creates a cultural expectation that loss is something to be hidden away, something that should be quickly dealt with and never spoken of again. This cultural silence prevents healing from taking place. Without the space to grieve openly, without the opportunity to express the profound love a mother feels for her lost child, healing becomes stunted. Grief can fester in isolation, leaving lasting psychological scars.

However, there's another more pervasive consequence of the church's silence about pre-birth loss—its impact on the broader cultural conversation around life, death, and the sanctity of unborn children. The silence and lack of acknowledgment surrounding pre-birth loss have indirectly played a role in perpetuating the abortion crisis we see in our culture today. When the church fails to address the sacredness of life before birth—especially in the context of miscarriage—it has inadvertently contributed to a devaluation of the life of the unborn in broader society. For years, the church has largely neglected to create a space where grief over the loss of a child before birth is publicly acknowledged and respected. By failing to recognize this form of loss, the church has left a void that society has filled with casual attitudes toward pre-birth life.

In a world where abortion has become an increasingly normalized part of our cultural fabric, the lack of acknowledgment of pre-birth loss within the church speaks volumes. The church's silence in this area fails to reinforce the inherent sanctity of every life from the moment of conception. When pre-birth loss is not given the respect it deserves, it can subtly reinforce the cultural notion that life at its earliest stages is disposable or insignificant. If the church won't recognize the grief of losing a child before birth, then why should society? This absence of consistent acknowledgment creates a fertile ground for a culture that treats unborn life as something that can be discarded without consequence. It contributes to the erosion of the understanding that every life is precious—no matter how small or brief it may be.

This is not to suggest that the church's silence alone is responsible for the rise in abortion rates, but it is clear that the lack of a strong, consistent, and compassionate message about the sanctity of life from conception has contributed to the normalization of abortion in our culture. When the church does not engage in the deep, hard conversations about the grief surrounding pre-birth loss, it fails to communicate the profound truth that every life—whether born or unborn—holds immeasurable worth in the eyes of God.

This silence also perpetuates a disconnect between faith and the real-world struggles that many mothers face when dealing with the pain of miscarriage or abortion. If a mother's grief over a miscarriage is not seen as legitimate by the church, then how can we expect the same community to support her in understanding the moral and spiritual implications of abortion? Without a clear, compassionate voice that upholds the value of all human life, the church inadvertently allows cultural attitudes to shape its teachings and response. By not fully embracing the mourning of pre-birth loss, the church undermines its own position on the sanctity of life.

What I needed wasn't to have my grief explained away or to be told that it was part of some grand plan I couldn't understand. I needed to be seen, to have my grief acknowledged for what it truly was—painful, sacred, and weighty. At my home church, I longed for more than these superficial words. I yearned for a community that could sit with me in my sorrow, that could validate my pain and acknowledge the sacredness of my unborn children's lives. I needed the church to walk alongside me—not to hurry me through the mourning process with empty phrases but to give me space to grieve, to remember, and to honor the lives that were lost.

Instead, I was often left feeling like my grief was something to be fixed, minimized, or ignored. The hardest part was realizing that these words weren't coming from a place of malice but from a place of love but a whole lot of discomfort. It seemed the church wasn't sure how to handle the depth of my loss, so it responded with trite words, hoping to bring comfort but only creating a chasm between my experience and the church's response. These well-intended platitudes left me feeling more misunderstood, more isolated in my grief. What I needed wasn't a quick fix; it was the sacred space to cry, to mourn, and to feel that my grief was seen and my child's life was valued.

When people rushed in with phrases like, "God has a plan" or "You'll see them again one day," they weren't wrong, but the truth was far more complex and much harder to digest in the midst of such profound loss. It wasn't that I didn't believe in God's plan or that I didn't long for a reunion with my children in heaven. It was that, in my grief, those words felt empty, like they were trying to wrap my pain in a neat little bow that didn't fit. I didn't need comforting words; I needed the church to show up with presence, to offer genuine empathy, and to sit with me in the silence of loss. I needed the church to understand that my children, though they never drew breath, were precious, and that my grief—no matter how difficult or uncomfortable—deserved to be met with respect and care, not glossed over with words that avoided the hard truths.

For grieving mothers, these shallow condolences don't provide solace—they create a wall. Instead of giving room for healing, they shut down the grief, leaving it unresolved. In attempting to make my pain go away, these words ignored the depth of what I was feeling, pushing my grief into the background. What I needed was not to be told what to believe about my child's life or my sorrow but to have the space to feel it, to speak their names, and to have my loss acknowledged as sacred. I longed for a place where my grief could be held with tenderness and where the church could meet me with the same deep compassion I was being called to offer others. It wasn't that I wanted answers; it was that I wanted to be seen, and to know that my child's life, however brief, was valued and sacred in the eyes of God and the community.

How can you, as a member of your faith community, create a space of healing and grace for those who have experienced the loss of an unborn child? What steps can your church take to break the silence and offer support for women navigating grief and loss?

Chapter Four

The Healing Power of Scripture

Grief is a deeply personal experience, one that varies from person to person but often feels as though it is a wound that cannot heal. For those grieving the loss of a preborn child, the heartache is layered—alongside the loss of a life, there is the unspoken weight of societal silence, the hidden grief that feels almost too tender to share. In such times, one might feel as though the world continues on, while their own world has stopped spinning. But there is one constant, a source of comfort, a balm for the aching heart—the healing power of Scripture.

For those walking through the deep grief of miscarriage or the weight of abortion, the pain is not just emotional but physical, as the loss can feel like a piece of oneself has been torn away. In such moments of darkness, Scripture shines like a beacon, offering words of comfort that have the power to heal even the deepest wounds. It's easy to think that the Bible, with its ancient words and distant setting, might not speak to the very real pain we experience today. But, in truth, God's Word is living and active, sharp and true, capable of reaching into the deepest parts of the human soul and offering hope.

The power of Scripture lies not just in its ancient wisdom but in the truth that it offers. God, the Creator of life, is present in our sorrow, and His Word reminds us that we do not grieve without hope. The Bible doesn't shy away from grief or pain—it acknowledges it, gives it a name, and then points to healing.

Psalm 34:18 is a beautiful reminder that God sees us in our deepest moments of sorrow: "The Lord is close to the brokenhearted and saves those who are crushed in spirit." There is a profound comfort in knowing that God is not distant, not removed from our pain, but that He draws near to us. He doesn't just observe from afar; He comes close, entering into the depths of our suffering with us. This verse is not a promise that the pain will go away immediately, but it is a promise that we will not face it alone. In our most broken moments, He is right there, holding us, comforting us, and offering us His peace.

At times, when we're in the depths of grief, the Scriptures may not feel like a quick fix. It can seem that the words on the page are distant or unhelpful, that the pain is too heavy to be lifted by mere verses. Yet, even when the healing feels slow, the act of turning to Scripture can itself be a form of healing. It reminds us that we are not forgotten, that God sees our pain, and He cares. Even if we cannot yet feel His presence, His Word serves as a reminder that He is there. Psalm 147:3 says, "He heals the brokenhearted and binds up their wounds." The act of turning to the Bible and reading through the pain, even when we don't feel like it, is itself a step toward healing. Healing is a process, and it often comes through the very act of remembering that God's promises are true, even when our feelings don't align with them.

One of the most comforting aspects of Scripture is the consistency of God's presence throughout all of life's trials. He is near in our moments of grief, our moments of joy, and even in our moments of waiting. There are so many moments in the Bible where we see God interacting with His people in their sorrow. We see it in the life of Jesus, who wept with those who mourned, even though He knew He would raise Lazarus from the dead. His tears were not a sign of weakness but of compassion, of His deep identification with human suffering. Jesus is not a distant Savior, but one who understands our pain intimately and walks with us through it.

One of the most tender invitations we receive from Jesus is in Matthew 11:28, where He says, "Come to me, all you who are weary and burdened, and I will give you rest." This invitation is not limited to those who have experienced physical weariness but extends to those who are spiritually, emotionally, and mentally burdened. Grief, in all its forms, is a heavy burden. And Jesus, in His great love, invites us to bring that burden to Him. He promises not just understanding, but rest—a rest for the soul that transcends the heaviness of life's burdens.

In those quiet, still moments when the world seems to fade away and the pain feels unbearable, it is in Scripture that we often find the clarity and peace that elude us in other places. In Isaiah 41:10, God reminds us of His constant presence and His promise to strengthen us, saying, "Do not fear, for I am with you; do not be dismayed, for I am your

God. I will strengthen you and help you; I will uphold you with my righteous right hand." The promise that God will strengthen and uphold us is not just for moments of physical weakness, but for emotional and spiritual weakness too. God knows the depths of our pain, and He promises to hold us, to strengthen us when we feel we cannot carry on.

There is a special healing that comes with knowing that God's Word is not just a set of principles or moral guidelines; it is the very voice of God speaking to us, offering us His comfort and His presence. And in the moments when we feel the deepest grief, it is the voice of God that can pierce through the silence and provide us with a peace that passes understanding. It is this peace that allows us to move forward, even in the midst of pain, trusting that our hearts will be healed in time.

The healing power of Scripture is not instantaneous, but it is sure. It is a healing that meets us where we are and works within us, slowly, steadily, as we allow it to. Even in our darkest moments, there is a promise of light. Even when the pain feels too much to bear, there is the hope of a future where all tears will be wiped away, where grief will no longer exist, and where the heartache of today will be replaced by the joy of a future in the presence of God. This hope does not ignore the pain we feel now, but it anchors us in the truth that our story does not end in sorrow.

The journey of grief is a long and winding road, but Scripture walks with us every step of the way, offering us healing, hope, and the promise that God is always with us, even in our deepest sorrow.

Take a moment to reflect on a verse or passage from this chapter that stood out to you. How can this Scripture speak into the pain you're carrying right now? Spend some time meditating on that verse, and let it remind you that God's Word is a source of comfort and healing, no matter how deep the grief.

Chapter Five

The Church's Role in Grief & Healing

The church is meant to be a place of comfort, refuge, and healing—a safe haven where those who are hurting can find solace and hope. For many who are grieving the loss of a pre-born child, whether through miscarriage or abortion, the church's response can mean the difference between healing and further isolation. Yet, unfortunately, the church has often struggled to address the grief of pre-birth loss, leaving many women feeling abandoned in their pain.

When a woman experiences the loss of a pre-born child, the grief she feels is often dismissed or minimized. Sometimes the silence surrounding miscarriage and abortion in the church is deafening. Many women feel that their grief is not significant enough to warrant acknowledgment, or they fear judgment from others, especially if their loss is tied to a decision they later regret. This silence creates a culture of shame and guilt, rather than one of compassion and healing.

The church's role in grief and healing should not be to offer easy answers or platitudes but to provide a safe space for grieving individuals to process their pain in community. It should be a place where sorrow is met with empathy, where women and families are encouraged to grieve fully, without fear of condemnation. As believers, we are called to offer comfort, but we are also called to walk alongside those who are hurting, to share in their grief, and to point them to the hope found in Jesus Christ.

In advocating for life, the church must also recognize that life is sacred not only in its beginning but also in its end. The grief of those who have lost pre-born children deserves the same attention, compassion, and support as any other form of loss. It's not enough to simply champion the sanctity of life without acknowledging the heartache that comes when that life is lost, whether through miscarriage or abortion. In fact, the church's failure to recognize this grief only compounds the pain many women feel.

When women suffer the loss of a child, they need more than just comforting words. They need a community that will walk with them through their pain, offering practical support, counseling, and the space to grieve fully. It is in the church's willingness to acknowledge the pain of pre-birth loss that healing begins. We are called to bear one another's burdens, to cry with those who cry and rejoice with those who rejoice. In doing so, we create an environment of grace, where healing can take place.

One of the most beautiful ways the church can support grieving families is by creating opportunities for women to publicly mourn their losses. Memorial services for pre-born children, baby dedications, and support groups specifically for those who have experienced miscarriage or abortion can help to validate the grief that many women feel. Such services and groups create an environment where women can grieve openly and receive the support they need, without fear of judgment or rejection.

Beyond specific services or groups, the church must foster a culture that embraces vulnerability and honesty. When women feel safe enough to share their stories of loss, they open the door for healing not only for themselves but for others who may be experiencing the same pain. This kind of openness builds a compassionate community—one where grief is not silenced but acknowledged and healed in the light of God's grace.

As the body of Christ, we are called to reflect the heart of God—a heart that is tender, compassionate, and full of mercy. The church's role in the healing process cannot be overstated. We are called to be a balm for the brokenhearted, a safe place for those who are suffering, and a beacon of hope in the midst of sorrow. The church's response to the grief of pre-birth loss must be one of compassion, understanding, and, above all, grace.

When the church fails to address this grief, it sends the message that the lives of pre-born children are not important, and that those who grieve their loss are somehow lesser. This silence perpetuates the stigma around miscarriage and abortion, making it harder for those who are suffering to find healing. But when the church chooses to stand in the gap, to provide comfort and compassion, it becomes a place where lives are truly transformed, where the grieving are embraced, and where the healing power of God's love is made manifest.

In the end, the church's role in grief and healing is simple: to be present, to offer comfort, and to lead those who are hurting to the only source of true healing—Jesus Christ.

Reflection Question: How can the church, as the body of Christ, better support those who are grieving in a way that reflects the compassion and love of Jesus? Reflect on what it would look like for your church to create a safe, healing space for those who are mourning and how you can be part of that change.

Author's Other Works

- Interrupted By Grace: Finding Jesus' Ministry in Motherhood